lonely planet
Kids

D0108343

first words
ITALIAN

TAXI

Illustrated by
Andy Mansfield & Sebastien Iwohn

hello
---
buongiorno

(bwon-jor-noh)

ACKNOWLEDGEMENTS

Publishing Director	Piers Pickard
Commissioning Editor,	Catharine Robertson
Assistant Editor	Christina Webb
Illustrators	Andy Mansfield
	Sebastien Iwohn
Designer	Andy Mansfield
Print production	Larissa Frost,
	Nigel Longuet

Published in March 2018 by Lonely Planet Global Ltd
CRN: 554153
ISBN: 978 1 78701 268 4
www.lonelyplanetkids.com
© Lonely Planet 2018
Printed in China

10 9 8 7 6 5 4 3 2 1

Lonely Planet Offices

AUSTRALIA
The Malt Store, Level 3, 551 Swanston St,
Carlton, Victoria 3053
T: 03 8379 8000

IRELAND
Unit E, Digital Court, The Digital Hub,
Rainsford St, Dublin 8

USA
124 Linden St, Oakland, CA 94607
T: 510 250 6400

UK
240 Blackfriars Rd, London SE1 8NW
T: 020 3771 5100

STAY IN TOUCH lonelyplanet.com/contact

MIX
Paper from
responsible sources
FSC™ C021741

Paper in this book is certified against the
Forest Stewardship Council™ standards.
FSC™ promotes environmentally responsible,
socially beneficial and economically viable
management of the world's forests.

ice cream
---
gelato

(jeh-lah-toh)

water
---
acqua
(a-kwa)

supermarket
supermercato

(soo-pair-mair-kah-toh)

shopping cart
carrello
(ka-rel-loh)

cat

---

gatto

(ga-toh)

bus

autobus

(ow-toh-boos)

dress
---
vestito

(ves-tee-toh)

dog
cane

(kah-neh)

banana
banana

(ba-nah-na)

carrot
---
carota

(ka-roh-ta)

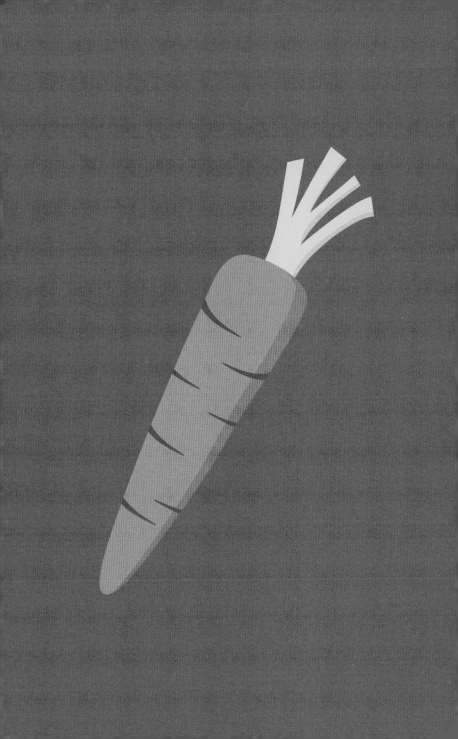

taxi
───
taxi
(tak-see)

t-shirt
---
maglietta

(mal-yeh-ta)

fish
---
pesce
(peh-sheh)

airplane
aereo
(ay-eh-ree-oh)

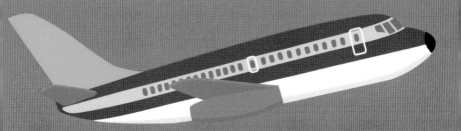

horse

---

cavallo

(ka-val-loh)

french fries
patatine fritte
(pa-ta-tee-neh free-teh)

swimming pool
piscina
(pee-shee-na)

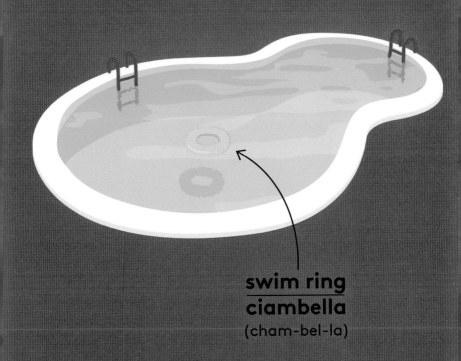

swim ring
ciambella
(cham-bel-la)

cheese
formaggio
(for-ma-joh)

towel

asciugamano

(a-shoo-ga-mah-noh)

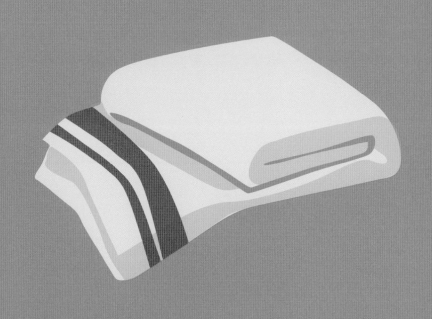

doctor
---
medico
(meh-dee-koh)

apple
mela

(meh-la)

worm
<hr>
verme
(vair-meh)

beach

spiaggia

(spee-ah-ja)

bicycle
bicicletta
(bee-chee-kleh-ta)

airport

aeroporto

(ay-roh-por-toh)

juice
---
succo

(soo-koh)

bakery
---
panetteria

(pa-net-eh-ree-a)

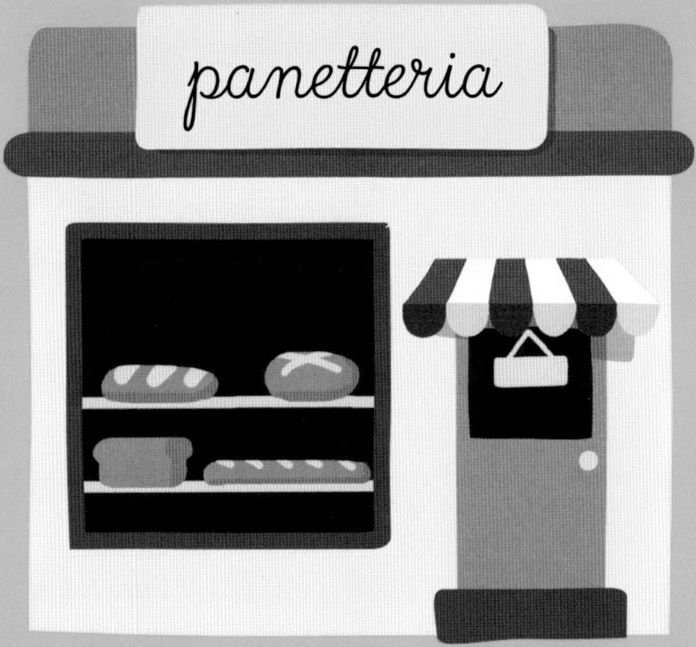
panetteria

shoes

---

scarpe

(skar-peh)

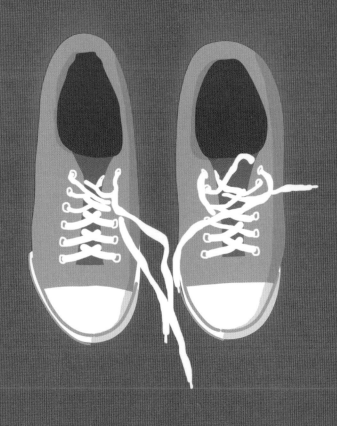

phone
telefono
(teh-leh-foh-noh)

post office
ufficio postale
(oo-fee-choh pos-tah-leh)

restaurant
---
ristorante
(rees-toh-ran-teh)

hotel

albergo

(al-bair-goh)

milk
---
latte
(la-teh)

chocolate
cioccolato
(cho-koh-lah-toh)

car
macchina
(mah-kee-na)

hat
cappello
(ka-pel-loh)

sunglasses
occhiali da sole
(o-kya-lee da soh-leh)

chicken
---
pollo
(po-loh)

train
treno
(tray-noh)

station
---
stazione
(stat-syo-neh)

clock
orologio
(or-oh-lo-joh)

toilet
gabinetto
(ga-bee-net-toh)

bed
---
letto

(leh-toh)

house
---
casa

(kah-za)

chimney
camino
(ka-mee-noh)

pants
pantaloni
(pan-ta-loh-nee)

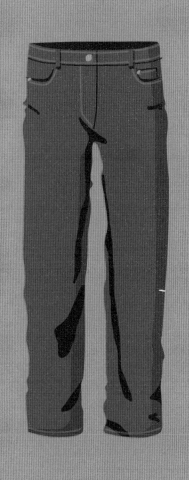

suitcase
---
valigia
(va-lee-jah)

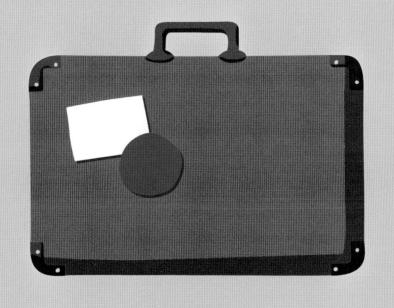

plate
piatto
(pee-a-toh)

knife
---
coltello

(kol-tel-loh)

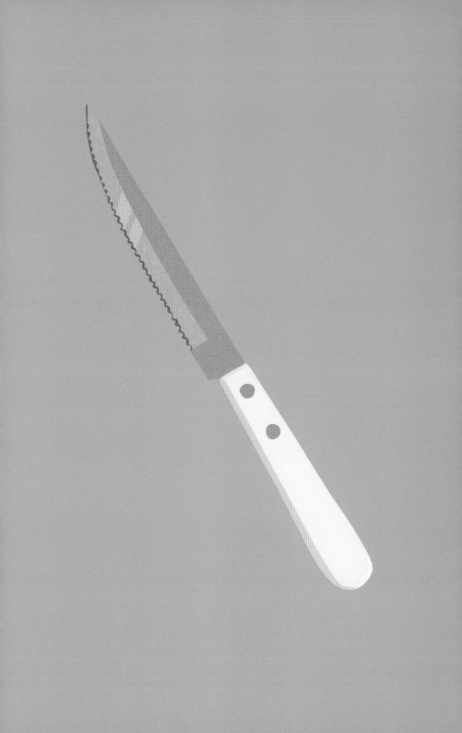

fork

---

forchetta

(for-ke-ta)

spoon
cucchiaio
(koo-kya-yoh)

computer

computer

(kom-pyoo-tair)

mouse
mouse del computer
(maus del kom-pyoo-tair)

book
libro
(lee-broh)

sandwich
---
tramezzino
(trah-meh-dzee-noh)

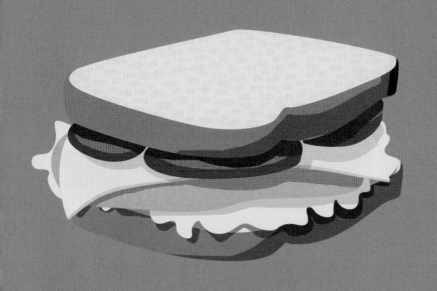

yes

sí

(see)

no
no
(no)

movie theater
cinema

(chee-neh-ma)

park

parco

(par-koh)

menu
---
menu

(meh-noo)

passport

passaporto

(pas-sa-por-toh)

police officer

polizia

(po-lee-tsee-a)

key
chiave
(kya-veh)

ticket
biglietto
(bee-lyet-oh)

pineapple

ananas

(ah-na-nas)

rain
pioggia
(pee-o-ja)

snow

---

neve

(neh-veh)

sun
___
sole
(soh-leh)

tree
---
albero

(al-beh-roh)

flower
fiore

(fee-or-reh)

cake

torta

(tor-ta)

cherry
ciliegia
(chil-yeh-jah)

ball

palla

(pal-la)

bird
---
uccello
(oo-chel-loh)

egg
uovo
(woh-voh)

umbrella
---
ombrello

(om-brel-loh)

rabbit
---
coniglio
(ko-nee-lyoh)

money
---
soldi

(sol-dee)

bank

---

banca

(ban-ka)

mouse / topo

(to-poh)

scarf

sciarpa

(shar-pa)

gloves
---
guanti
(gwan-tee)

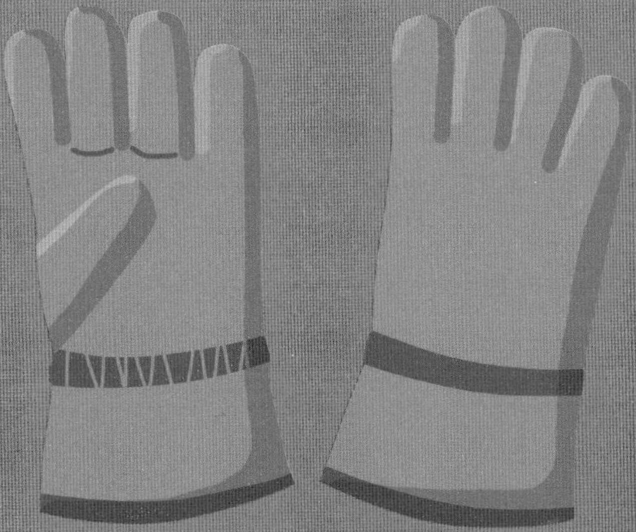

coat

---

cappotto

(kap-pot-toh)

hospital

ospedale

(os-peh-dah-leh)

chair
---
sedia

(seh-dya)

table
---
tavolo

(tah-voh-loh)

toothbrush
---
spazzolino da denti

(spat-soh-lee-noh
da den-tee)

toothpaste

dentifricio

(den-tee-free-choh)

sunscreen

crema solare

(kray-ma so-lah-reh)

lion
---
leone
(lay-oh-neh)

elephant
elefante
(el-eh-fan-teh)

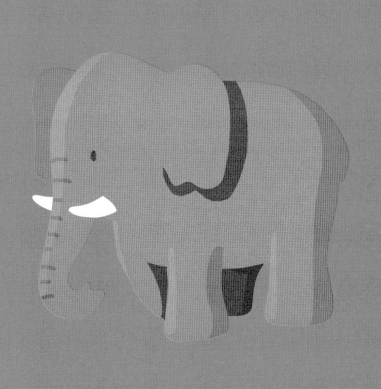

monkey
scimmia

(shee-mya)

spider

ragno

(rah-nyoh)

burger
hamburger
(am-boor-gair)

pen

penna

(pen-na)

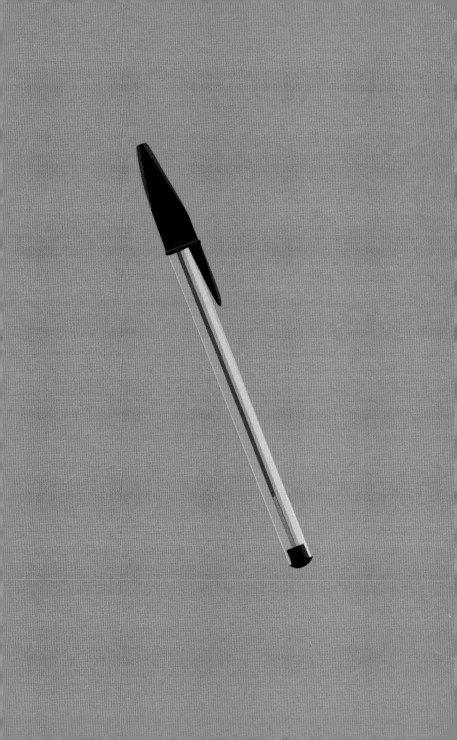

door

---

porta

(por-ta)

window
finestra

(fee-nes-tra)

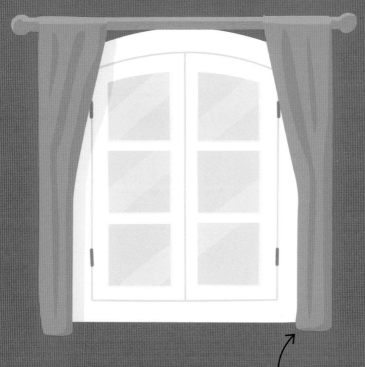

curtain
tenda
(ten-da)

tent

---

tenda

(ten-da)

church
chiesa
(kyeh-za)

tomato
---
pomodoro
(poh-moh-dor-oh)

moon
---
luna

(loo-na)

stars

stelle

(stel-leh)

postcard
cartolina
(kar-toh-lee-na)

stamp

francobollo

(fran-koh-boh-loh)

boat

---

barca

(bar-ka)

goodbye
arrivederci
(a-ree-veh-der-chee)